❋ Stitch a ❋ Beaded Garden

Sparkling beads bloom into flowers on these stunning samplers and mini motifs. Stitched over two threads on 28-count evenweave fabric, each project uses colorful seed beads. You can create garden favorites such as bleeding hearts, carnations, clematis, dahlias, peonies, and zinnias. You'll even find fresh grapes to stitch! Bugle beads and Cross Stitches appear on a few of the designs, and a simple Backstitch alphabet is provided so you can sign and date each project. The smaller designs make lovely framed pieces and keepsake greeting cards. If you'd prefer to Cross Stitch any of these designs, DMC and Sullivans floss substitutions are included. Now you can stitch a lovely decorator piece for your home, or present someone special with blossoms they will cherish forever!

jo.ann loveland   Tues aug 28, 2012

❋ Table of Contents ❋

LEISURE ARTS, INC.
Little Rock, Arkansas

A Letter from Sharon

Photo by Tonya Nobelen

My love of flowers comes from a childhood spent in my parent's garden. I was born in New Zealand in the 1950's. Like most of our neighbors, my parents kept a vegetable garden to feed the family and grew flowers to feed the soul. I was even allowed my own garden to plant whatever I wished. The variety of flowers in those gardens always held my attention with their form, their texture, and their perfumes.

Inside the house, there was sewing—not only to help clothe the family, but also to decorate the home. I was encouraged to sew and I have done so ever since I could hold a needle. I was eleven years old when I began stitching in school on some Aida cloth. I sewed the sides together to form a sewing bag to hold the rest of the year's projects.

Time marched on; I went to work and then had children. While I did lots of sewing and knitting, I wasn't able to do much in the area of embroidery in those years. Now that I have a little more time, I have gone back to it. I have found that I am particularly attracted to samplers. They take many forms and the embroiderer can leap from one idea to another. I looked at many historic examples and made a few reproductions. I also realized that the workbag—done at school all those years ago—had in fact been a sampler! I unpicked the side seams, gently washed it, and proudly had it framed.

Ten years later, a dear aunt of mine enthusiastically informed me that she also had an old sampler stored away. It transpired that it was one stitched by my great-great-great-grandmother in 1839 at age 10. Born in Birmingham, England, this ancestor had kept it as one of her treasured possessions when she came to New Zealand in 1864 with her husband and seven children. The sampler has been passed down through the women of the family, and it was quite a moving moment when I first saw it.

When traveling overseas with my husband, I was drawn to some of the old beadwork in the museums. It gave stitching another dimension and made it come alive in a quite different way. Gradually it dawned on me: All of these things could be combined—embroidery, beadwork, samplers, and gardens. Since then, I have spent many happy hours designing and stitching the following beaded samplers and florals. I hope you have as many happy hours stitching them for yourself and your loved ones.

—*Sharon Maxwell Kendall Perry*

PS: I also love to quilt! If you enjoy machine quilting, please visit HouseOfCreations.biz, where you can view and purchase a wide variety of quilting patterns.

Zinnia

This plant gives the impression of little groups of soldiers marching around the edge of the garden — so stiff and straight with little bobble heads on the end of each stem.

Chart for Zinnia Rectangle, shown here, is on pages 24 and 25. Charts for two other sizes are on pages 21-23.

Chart is on pages 26 and 27.

Carnation Band

How fascinated I was when I first saw orange and gold carnations! When I was stitching them, I rediscovered how oranges and golds look completely lifeless without the little bit of blue.

Chart is on pages 28-31.

Clematis

Once established, clematis plants just climb everywhere and more often than not have to be brought into check quite regularly. In New Zealand, one variety was not tamed in time and has become invasive. It nevertheless looks magnificent when in flower, and can be seen for miles.

Star Daisy

These little stars are long lasting and really put on a show.

Chart is on pages 32 and 33.

Canterbury Bells

Canterbury Bells are very tall and formal, usually in shades of blue, pink or white. The name "Cup and Saucer" refers to the double strain which has an extra round of petals under each "bell."

Chart is on pages 34 and 35.

Chart is on pages 36 and 37.

Bleeding Hearts

For many, many years, this plant's name intrigued me. It was such a sad name — but the plant was so lovely.

Chart is on pages 38-41.

Alphabet Web

Most of us don't enjoy spiders all that much, but they do have to be admired for their wonderful webs — and their tenacity. A web can be destroyed one day, and by the next it is back up and running. Webs are made everywhere in the garden — in trees, amongst flowers, under seats! Covered with morning dew, they look just like strings of beads.

Sweet Pea

At the back of our garden along the wall was a long row of sweet peas. Their sweet perfume astounded me. I wasn't aware of it at the time, but Mother was growing them for the local florist. This would pay for her visit to the hair salon. Even to this day, the perfume of sweet peas turns my head!

Chart is on pages 42 and 43.

Pinks

How surprising is the fragrance of these little beauties — like cloves! Now where did that come from? How unexpected!

Chart is on pages 44-46.

Mallow

This name always reminds me of marshmallows. And fair enough too, they usually come in soft pinks and white.

Chart is on page 47.

Chart is on pages 48 and 49.

Peony

Life started for me at the warm end of New Zealand — the northern part of the North Island. I loved peonies when they arrived in the shops, saddened only that I couldn't grow them in our warmer clime. However, when we moved to Dunedin — at the southern end of the South Island — I was thrilled to be able to grow them myself.

Chart is on pages 50-53.

The Vineyard

Now that she is well into her retirement, Mother is living on a 2¹/₂ acre block which has been carved off the corner of a vineyard. She has created her own "little slice of heaven" with a most wonderful garden. It has pansies and forget-me-nots happily growing with the roses under the fruit trees and around the hen run. She spends many hours in this "heaven" doing her calligraphy.

Waterlily

How can flowers grow in the middle of ponds? To this day, this still amazes me.

Chart is on pages 54 and 55.

Dahlia

Impatiens

Galicia Rose

Forget-Me-Not

Charts are on pages 17-20.

Dahlia

Each design was stitched over 2 fabric threads on a 5½" x 6½" piece of Zweigart® Antique White Lugana Evenweave (28 count). Beads were attached using 2 strands of floss that matches the fabric. The larger version (design size 1½" x 2½", shown on page 16) was framed in a 2" x 3" purchased frame. The smaller version (design size 1½" x 2¼", shown on page 60) was placed in a card. For card, follow **Making a Card**, page 59.

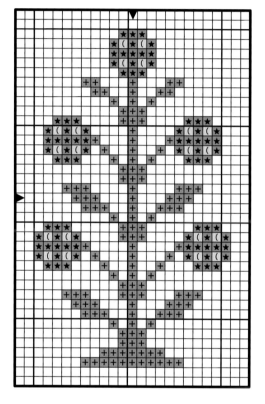 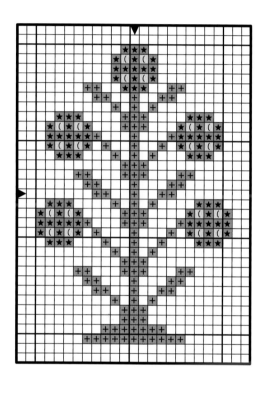

Stitch Count:
Large (21w x 35h)
Small (21w x 31h)

SYMBOL	MILL HILL	COLOR	QUANTITY (Large)	(Small)
+	00167 Seed Bead	Christmas Green	130	114
★	02034 Seed Bead	Autumn Flame	85	85
(	02039 Seed Bead	Matte Maize	20	20

FLOSS SUBSTITUTION KEY

To stitch this design in floss only, replace each seed bead with a Cross Stitch. Use 2 strands of floss.

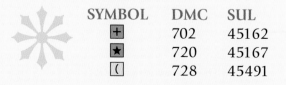

SYMBOL	DMC	SUL
+	702	45162
★	720	45167
(	728	45491

Impatiens

Each design was stitched over 2 fabric threads on a $5^1/2$" x $6^1/2$" piece of Zweigart® Antique White Lugana Evenweave (28 count). Beads were attached using 2 strands of floss that matches the fabric. The larger version (design size $1^1/2$" x $2^1/2$", shown on page 16) was framed in a 2" x 3" purchased frame. The smaller versions (design size $1^1/2$" x $2^1/4$", shown on page 60) were placed in cards. For card, follow **Making a Card**, page 59.

Stitch Count:
Large (21w x 35h)
Small (21w x 31h)

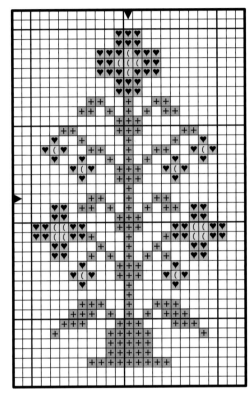 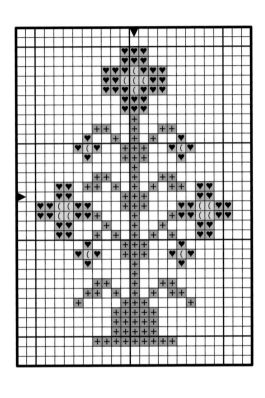

SYMBOL	MILL HILL	COLOR	QUANTITY	
			(Large)	(Small)
+	00167 Seed Bead	Christmas Green	128	94
(	00557 Seed Bead	Old Gold	19	17
♥	02085 Seed Bead*	Brilliant Orchid	84	76

*For pink impatiens, use 02012 Seed Bead, Royal Plum.

FLOSS SUBSTITUTION KEY

To stitch this design in floss only, replace each seed bead with a Cross Stitch. Use 2 strands of floss.

SYMBOL	DMC	SUL
+	702	45162
(	3821	45418
♥	3837†	45435†

†For pink impatiens, use DMC 3805 or Sullivans 45402.

Forget-Me-Not

Each design was stitched over 2 fabric threads on a $5^1/_2$" x $6^1/_2$" piece of Zweigart® Antique White Lugana Evenweave (28 count). Beads were attached using 2 strands of floss that matches the fabric. The larger version (design size $1^1/_2$" x $2^1/_2$", shown on page 16) was framed in a 2" x 3" purchased frame. The smaller version (design size $1^1/_2$" x $2^1/_4$", shown on page 60) was placed in a card. For card, follow **Making a Card**, page 59.

Stitch Count:
Large (21w x 35h)
Small (21w x 31h)

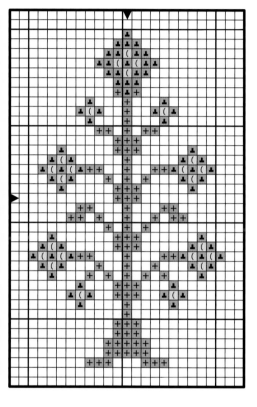
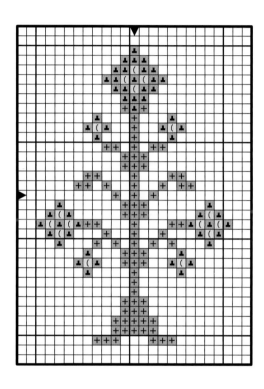

SYMBOL	MILL HILL	COLOR	QUANTITY	
			(Large)	(Small)
(	02052 Seed Bead	Dark Coral	24	16
+	02098 Seed Bead	Pine Green	95	81
⚐	02103 Seed Bead	Periwinkle	73	55

FLOSS SUBSTITUTION KEY

To stitch this design in floss only, replace each seed bead with a Cross Stitch. Use 2 strands of floss.

SYMBOL	DMC	SUL
(	356	45079
+	937	45279
⚐	791	45202

Galicia Rose

Each design was stitched over 2 fabric threads on a 5¹/₂" x 6¹/₂" piece of Zweigart® Antique White Lugana Evenweave (28 count). Beads were attached using 2 strands of floss that matches the fabric. The larger version (design size 1¹/₂" x 2¹/₂", shown on page 16) was framed in a 2" x 3" purchased frame. The smaller version (design size 1¹/₂" x 2¹/₄", shown on page 60) was placed in a card. For card, follow **Making a Card**, page 59.

Stitch Count:
Large (21w x 35h)
Small (21w x 31h)

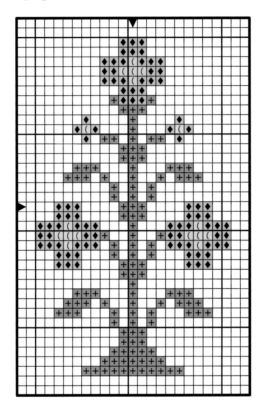

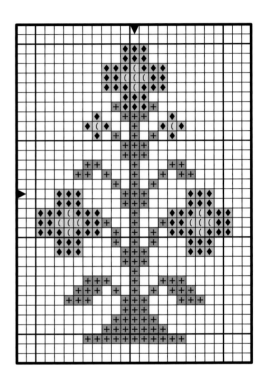

SYMBOL	MILL HILL	COLOR	QUANTITY	
			(Large)	(Small)
(	02001 Seed Bead	Pearl	17	17
+	02098 Seed Bead	Pine Green	120	104
◆	03057 Seed Bead	Cherry Sorbet	92	92

FLOSS SUBSTITUTION KEY

To stitch this design in floss only, replace each seed bead with a Cross Stitch. Use 2 strands of floss.

SYMBOL	DMC	SUL
(	677	45157
+	937	45279
◆	760	45191

Zinnia (Small Square)

Zinnia Rectangle is shown on page 4. This smaller version was designed to fit a 3¹/₂" x 3¹/₂" frame. It was stitched over 2 fabric threads on a 7" x 7" piece of Zweigart® Black Cashel Linen® (28 count). The design size is 2³/₄" x 2³/₄". Beads were attached using 2 strand of floss that matches the fabric. The design was custom framed.

Stitch Count:
Small (37w x 38h)

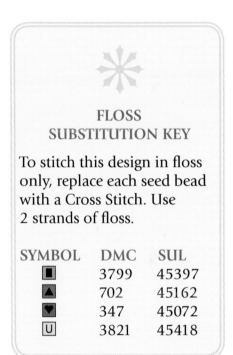

FLOSS SUBSTITUTION KEY

To stitch this design in floss only, replace each seed bead with a Cross Stitch. Use 2 strands of floss.

SYMBOL	DMC	SUL
■	3799	45397
▲	702	45162
♥	347	45072
U	3821	45418

SYMBOL	MILL HILL	COLOR	QUANTITY
■	00081 Seed Bead	Jet	156
▲	00167 Seed Bead	Christmas Green	79
♥	02075 Seed Bead	Grenadine	164
U	02011 Seed Bead	Victorian Gold	50

Stitch Count:
Large (57w x 57h)

Zinnia (Large Square)

Zinnia Rectangle is shown on page 4. This version was designed to fit a 5" x 5" frame. It was stitched over 2 fabric threads on a $10^1/_2$" x $10^1/_2$" piece of Zweigart® Raw Cashel Linen® (28 count). The design size is $4^1/_8$" x $4^1/_8$". Beads were attached using 2 strands of floss that matches the fabric. If desired, Backstitch the stitcher's name and year stitched using 1 strand of floss in desired color and the small alphabet on page 56. The design was custom framed.

SYMBOL	MILL HILL	COLOR	QUANTITY
■	00081 Seed Bead	Jet	161
☰	00221 Seed Bead	Bronze	351
♥	02012 Seed Bead	Royal Plum	164
U	02019 Seed Bead	Crystal Honey	62
▲	03035 Seed Bead	Royal Green	92

FLOSS SUBSTITUTION KEY

To stitch this design in floss only, replace each seed bead with a Cross Stitch. Use 2 strands of floss.

SYMBOL	DMC	SUL
■	3799	45397
☰	434	45095
♥	3803	45400
U	745	45186
▲	991	45311

Stitch Count:
(55w x 83h)

Zinnia (Rectangle)

The design, shown on page 4, was stitched over 2 fabric threads on a 10" x 12" piece of Zweigart® Raw Cashel Linen® (28 count). The design size is 4" x 6". Beads were attached using 2 strands of floss that matches the fabric. If desired, Backstitch the stitcher's name and year stitched using 1 strand of floss in desired color and the small alphabet on page 56. The design was custom framed.

SYMBOL	MILL HILL	COLOR	QUANTITY
▣	00081 Seed Bead	Jet	182
▤	00221 Seed Bead	Bronze	441
♥	02012 Seed Bead	Royal Plum	296
U	02019 Seed Bead	Crystal Honey	109
▲	03035 Seed Bead	Royal Green	225

FLOSS SUBSTITUTION KEY

To stitch this design in floss only, replace each seed bead with a Cross Stitch. Use 2 strands of floss.

SYMBOL	DMC	SUL
▣	3799	45397
▤	434	45095
♥	3803	45400
U	745	45186
▲	991	45311

Carnation Band

The design, shown on page 5, was stitched over 2 fabric threads on a 9¹/₂" x 15" piece of Zweigart® Flax Cashel Linen® (28 count). The design size is 3¹/₈" x 8⁷/₈". Two strands of floss were used for Cross Stitch. Dark Basil beads were attached using 2 strands of dark green floss. All other beads were attached using 2 strands of floss that matches the fabric. If desired, Backstitch the stitcher's name and year stitched using 1 strand of floss in desired color and the small alphabet on page 56. The design was custom framed.

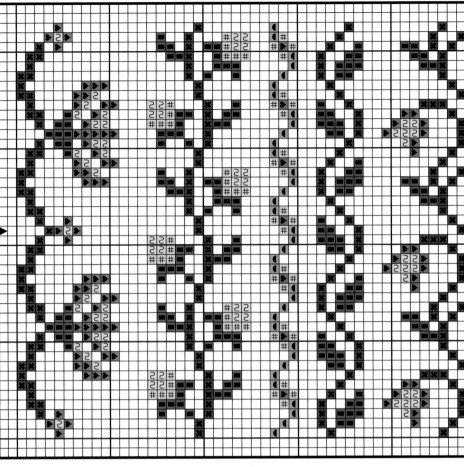

Stitch Count:
(43w x 123h)

SYMBOL		DMC	COLOR
X	✕	936	dark green

	SUL	COLOR	QUANTITY
	45278	dark green	

SYMBOL		BEAD	COLOR	QUANTITY
2		02019 Mill Hill Seed Bead	Crystal Honey	152
#		02043 Mill Hill Seed Bead	Matte Pomegranate	116
■		02049 Mill Hill Seed Bead	Dark Basil	426
◑		02087 Mill Hill Seed Bead	Shimmering Sea	213
▶		03038 Mill Hill Seed Bead	Antique Ginger	281
▯		2mm bugle bead*	dark green	18
▨		Indicates repeated row		

*Two Dark Basil seed beads may be used in place of each bugle bead.

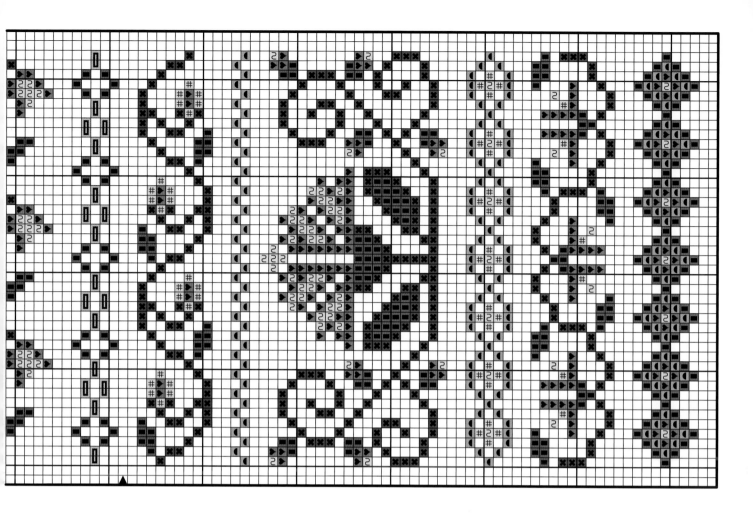

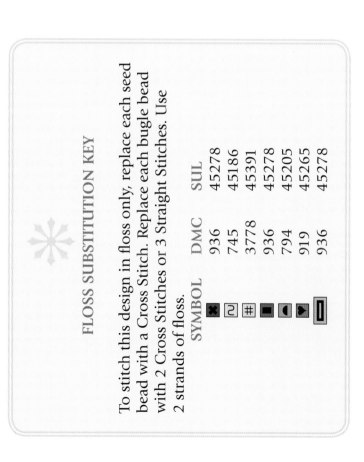

FLOSS SUBSTITUTION KEY

To stitch this design in floss only, replace each seed bead with a Cross Stitch. Replace each bugle bead with 2 Cross Stitches or 3 Straight Stitches. Use 2 strands of floss.

SYMBOL	DMC	SUL
✖	936	45278
⧖	745	45186
#	3778	45391
■	936	45278
◖	794	45205
▶	919	45265
🟦	936	45278

27

Clematis

The design, shown on page 6, was stitched over 2 fabric threads on a 15" x 13" piece of Zweigart® Flax Cashel Linen® (28 count). The design size is 8⁷/₈" x 6⁷/₈". Two strands of floss were used for Cross Stitch. Beads were attached using 2 strands of floss that matches the fabric. Personalize the design by adding the stitchers initials and the year stitched using Heather Mauve seed beads and the large alphabet on page 56. The design was framed in an 8" x 10" purchased frame.

Stitch Count:
(123w x 95h)

SYMBOL	MILL HILL	COLOR	QUANTITY
■	00081 Seed Bead	Jet	151
U	02001 Seed Bead	Pearl	11
★	02023 Seed Bead	Root Beer	340
+	02024 Seed Bead	Heather Mauve	344*
◆	02025 Seed Bead	Heather	659
I	02077 Seed Bead	Brilliant Magenta	44
C	03059 Seed Bead	Green Velvet	666
▬	72051 Small Bugle Bead	Royal Mauve	12
▨	Indicates repeated row		

*Does not include personalization (initials and year).

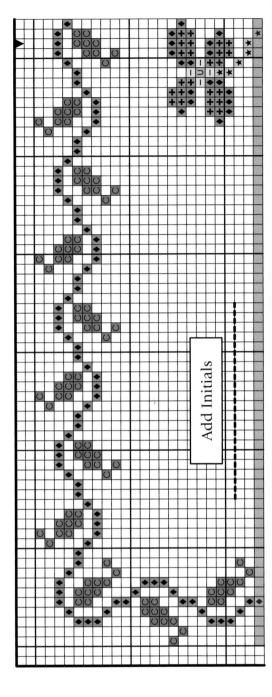

Add Initials

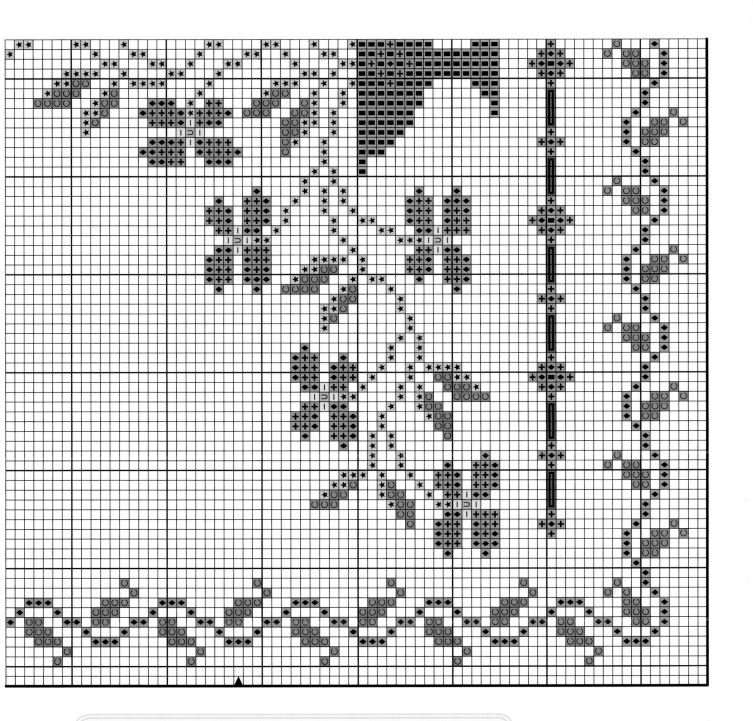

Chart is continued on pages 30 and 31.

FLOSS SUBSTITUTION KEY

To stitch this design in floss only, replace each seed bead with a Cross Stitch. Replace each bugle bead with 4 Cross Stitches or 3 Straight Stitches. Use 2 strands of floss.

SYMBOL	DMC	SUL
■	3799	45397
U	677	45157
★	3826	45423
+	3042	45327
◆	3740	45371
I	915	45262
C	3346	45343
▯	3041	45326

29

Clematis (continued from pages 28 and 29)

SYMBOL	MILL HILL	COLOR
■	00081 Seed Bead	Jet
∪	02001 Seed Bead	Pearl
★	02023 Seed Bead	Root Beer
✚	02024 Seed Bead	Heather Mauve
◆	02025 Seed Bead	Heather
—	02077 Seed Bead	Brilliant Magenta
C	03059 Seed Bead	Green Velvet
▮	72051 Small Bugle Bead	Royal Mauve
▮	Indicates repeated rows	

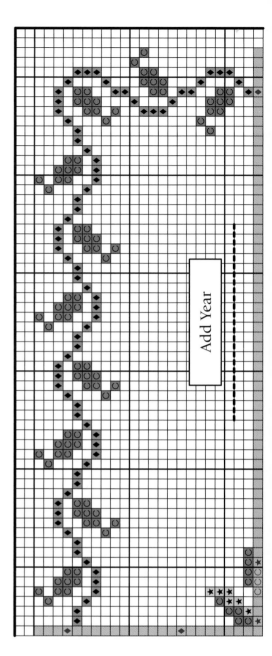

Add Year

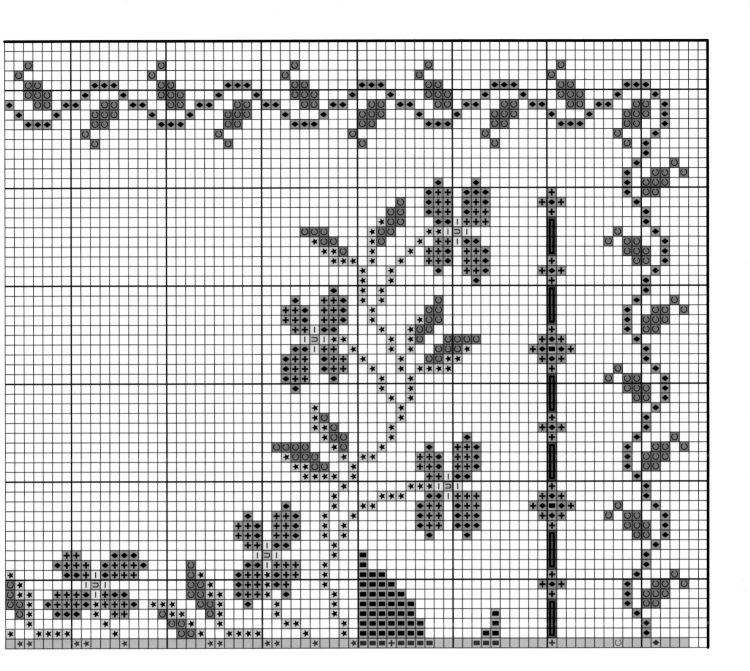

Star Daisy

The design, shown on page 7, was stitched over 2 fabric threads on a 9$^1/_2$" x 11" piece of Zweigart® Flax Cashel Linen® (28 count). The design, shown on lower left, was also stitched on Zweigart® Black Cashel Linen® (28 count). The design size is 3$^1/_8$" x 4$^3/_4$". Beads were attached using 2 strands of floss that matches the fabric. If desired, Backstitch the stitcher's name and year stitched using 1 strand of floss in desired color and the small alphabet on page 56. Each version was framed in a 4" x 6" purchased frame.

FLAX LINEN

SYMBOL	MILL HILL	COLOR	QUANTITY
■	00081 Seed Bead	Jet	201
▲	00332 Seed Bead	Emerald	309
U	02011 Seed Bead	Victorian Gold	110
♥	03003 Seed Bead	Antique Cranberry	240

BLACK LINEN

SYMBOL	MILL HILL	COLOR	QUANTITY
■	00081 Seed Bead	Jet	201
▲	00167 Seed Bead	Christmas Green	309
U	02011 Seed Bead	Victorian Gold	110
♥	02034 Seed Bead	Autumn Flame	240

Stitch Count:
(43w x 66h)

FLOSS SUBSTITUTION KEY

To stitch this design in floss only, replace each seed bead with a Cross Stitch. Use 2 strands of floss.

FLAX LINEN				BLACK LINEN		
SYMBOL	DMC	SUL		SYMBOL	DMC	SUL
■	3799	45397		■	3799	45397
▲	890	45243		▲	702	45162
U	3821	45418		U	3821	45418
♥	347	45072		♥	720	45167

Stitch Count:
(43w x 68h)

Canterbury Bells

The design, shown on page 8, was stitched over 2 fabric threads on a 9^1/$_2$" x 11" piece of Zweigart® Raw Cashel Linen® (28 count). The design, shown on lower left, was also stitched on Zweigart® Black Cashel Linen® (28 count). The design size is 3^1/$_8$" x 4^7/$_8$". Beads were attached using 2 strands of floss that matches the fabric. If desired, Backstitch the stitcher's name and year stitched using 1 strand of floss in desired color and the small alphabet on page 56. Each version was framed in a 4" x 6" purchased frame.

RAW LINEN

SYMBOL	MILL HILL	COLOR	QUANTITY
▉	00081 Seed Bead	Jet	215
U	02019 Seed Bead	Crystal Honey	67
▲	02020 Seed Bead	Creme de Mint	302
✚	03053 Seed Bead	Purple Passion	319

BLACK LINEN

SYMBOL	MILL HILL	COLOR	QUANTITY
▉	00081 Seed Bead	Jet	215
▲	00167 Seed Bead	Christmas Green	302
U	02040 Seed Bead	Light Amber	67
✚	02089 Seed Bead	Brilliant Sea Blue	319

FLOSS SUBSTITUTION KEY

To stitch this design in floss only, replace each seed bead with a Cross Stitch. Replace each bugle bead with 2 Cross Stitches or 3 Straight Stitches. Use 2 strands of floss.

RAW LINEN				BLACK LINEN		
SYMBOL	DMC	SUL		SYMBOL	DMC	SUL
▉	3799	45397		▉	3799	45397
U	745	45186		▲	702	45162
▲	909	45257		U	3829	45426
✚	3746	45373		✚	3765	45382

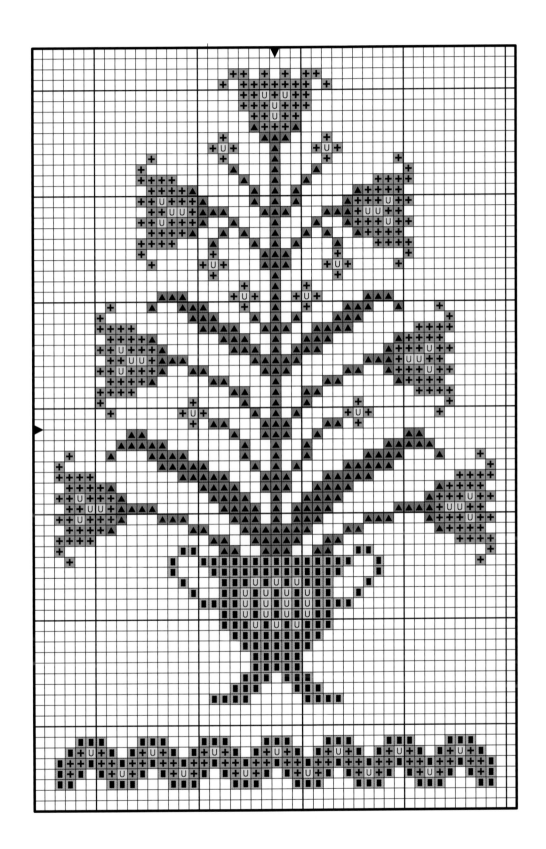

Stitch Count:
(55w x 83h)

Bleeding Hearts

The design, shown on page 9, was stitched over 2 fabric threads on a 10" x 12" piece of Zweigart® Raw Cashel Linen® (28 count). The design size is 4" x 6". Beads were attached using 2 strands of floss that matches the fabric. If desired, Backstitch the stitcher's name and year stitched using 1 strand of floss in desired color and the small alphabet on page 56. The design was framed in a 5" x 7 purchased frame.

SYMBOL	MILL HILL	COLOR	QUANTITY
■	00081 Seed Bead	Jet	161
▲	00332 Seed Bead	Emerald	275
♥	03003 Seed Bead	Antique Cranberry	556
T	03051 Seed Bead	Misty	187

FLOSS SUBSTITUTION KEY

To stitch this design in floss only, replace each seed bead with a Cross Stitch. Use 2 strands of floss.

SYMBOL	DMC	SUL
■	3799	45397
▲	890	45243
♥	347	45072
T	761	45192

Alphabet Web

The design, shown on page 10, was stitched over 2 fabric threads on a 15" x 18" piece of Zweigart® Flax Cashel Linen® (28 count). The design size is $8^5/_8$" x $11^3/_4$". Beads were attached using 2 strands of floss that matches the fabric. Personalize the design by adding the stitcher's initials and the year stitched using a mixture of Claret and Cognac seed beads and the large alphabet on page 56. The design was custom framed.

Stitch Count:
(120w x 164h)

SYMBOL	MILL HILL	COLOR	QUANTITY
6	00374 Seed Bead	Rainbow	1,883
♥	02012 Seed Bead	Royal Plum	710
U	02019 Seed Bead	Crystal Honey	44
5	02024 Seed Bead	Heather Mauve	326
★	{ 03033 Seed Bead*	Claret	1,060†
	{ 03036 Seed Bead*	Cognac	
✖	03035 Seed Bead	Royal Green	874
▭	70374 Small Bugle Bead	Rainbow	63
▢	Indicates repeated row		

*Use a mixture of 03033 and 03036 seed beads.
†Does not include personalization (initials and year).

FLOSS SUBSTITUTION KEY

To stitch this design in floss only, replace each seed bead with a Cross Stitch. Replace each bugle bead with 4 Cross Stitches or 3 Straight Stitches. Use 2 strands of floss.

SYMBOL	DMC	SUL
6	550	45123
♥	3803	45400
U	745	45186
5	3042	45327
★	355	45078
✖	986	45307
▭	550	45123

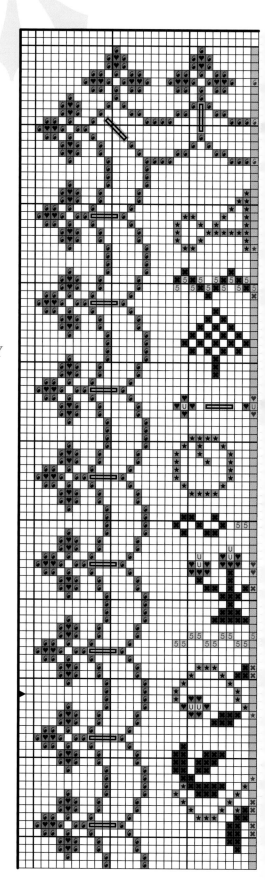

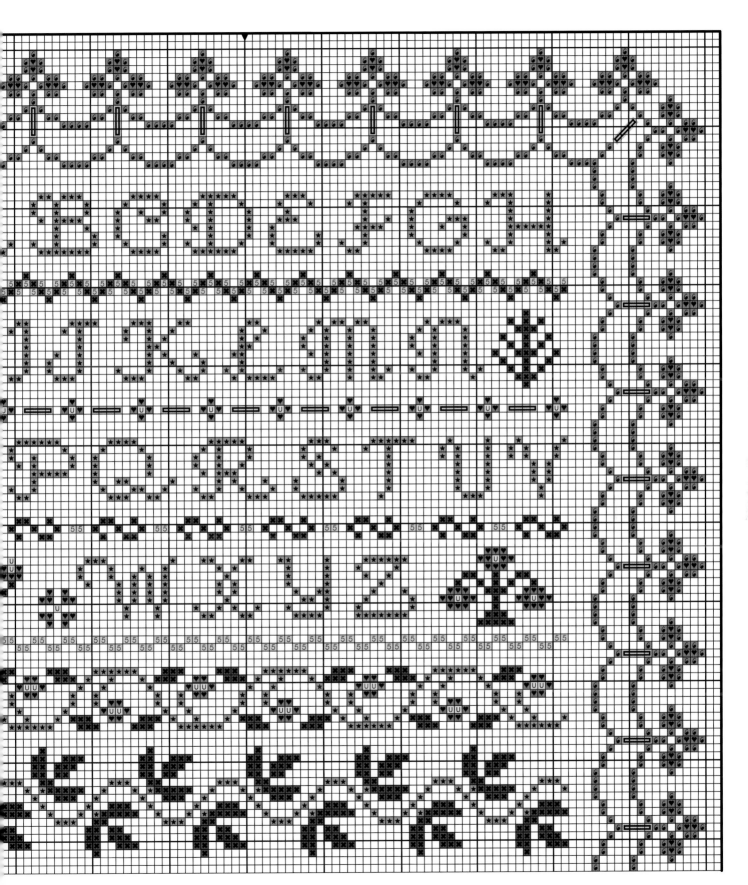

Chart is continued on pages 40 and 41.

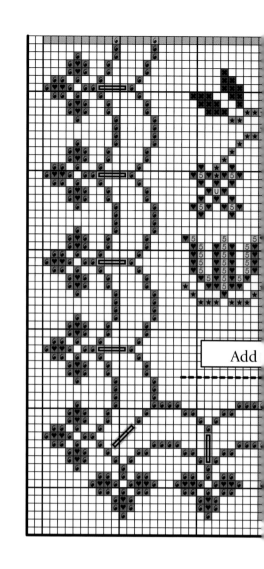

Add

Alphabet Web (continued from pages 38 and 39)

SYMBOL	MILL HILL	COLOR
6	00374 Seed Bead	Rainbow
♥	02012 Seed Bead	Royal Plum
U	02019 Seed Bead	Crystal Honey
5	02024 Seed Bead	Heather Mauve
★	{ 03033 Seed Bead*	Claret
	{ 03036 Seed Bead*	Cognac
✖	03035 Seed Bead	Royal Green
▭	70374 Small Bugle Bead	Rainbow
▨	Indicates repeated rows	

*Use of mixture of 03033 and 03036 seed beads.

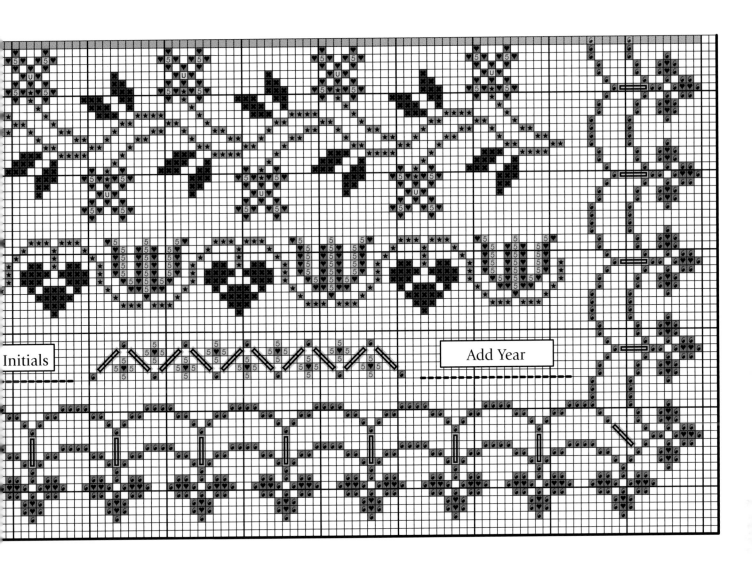

Initials

Add Year

Stitch Count:
(43w x 85h)

Sweet Pea

The design, shown on page 11, was stitched over 2 fabric threads on a 9$^{1}/_{2}$" x 12$^{1}/_{2}$" piece of Zweigart® Ivory Lugana Evenweave (28 count). The design size is 3$^{1}/_{8}$" x 6$^{1}/_{8}$". Two strands of floss were used for Cross Stitch. Beads were attached using 2 strands of floss that matches the fabric. If desired, Backstitch the stitcher's name and year stitched using 1 strand of floss in desired color and small alphabet on page 56. The design was custom framed.

X	DMC	SUL	COLOR
C	523	45119	green

SYMBOL	MILL HILL	COLOR	QUANTITY
◖	00168 Seed Bead	Sapphire	210
✛	02005 Seed Bead	Dusty Rose	235
∿	02019 Seed Bead	Crystal Honey	154
▲	03055 Seed Bead	Bay Leaf	379

FLOSS SUBSTITUTION KEY

To stitch this design in floss only, replace each seed bead with a Cross Stitch. Use 2 strands of floss.

SYMBOL	DMC	SUL
C	523	45119
◖	809	45214
✛	3354	45347
∿	745	45186
▲	3052	45332

Pinks

The design, shown on page 12, was stitched over 2 fabric threads on a 12" x 16" piece of Zweigart® Raw Cashel Linen® (28 count). The design size is 5³/₄" x 9³/₄". Two strands of floss were used for Cross Stitch. Dark Basil beads were attached using 2 strands of dark green floss. All other beads were attached using 2 strands of floss that matches the fabric. If desired, Backstitch the stitcher's name and year stitched using 1 strand of floss in desired color and the small alphabet on page 56. The design was custom framed.

Stitch Count:
(79w x 135h)

X	DMC	SUL	COLOR	
✖	936	45278	dark green	

SYMBOL	BEAD		COLOR	QUANTITY
♥	02012 Mill Hill Seed Bead		Royal Plum	470
U	02019 Mill Hill Seed Bead		Crystal Honey	334
5	02024 Mill Hill Seed Bead		Heather Mauve	416
▮	02049 Mill Hill Seed Bead		Dark Basil	1,014
◖	03062 Mill Hill Seed Bead		Blue Velvet	243
▭	2mm bugle bead*		dark green	28
▪	Indicates repeated row			

*Two Dark Basil seed beads may be used in place of each bugle bead.

Chart is continued on page 46.

FLOSS SUBSTITUTION KEY

To stitch this design in floss only, replace each seed bead with a Cross Stitch. Replace each bugle bead with 2 Cross Stitches or 3 Straight Stitches. Use 2 strands of floss.

SYMBOL	DMC	SUL
✖	936	45278
▼	3803	45400
U	745	45186
5	3042	45327
◼	936	45278
◉	797	45207
▭	936	45278

Pinks (continued from pages 44 and 45)

X	DMC	SUL	COLOR
⊠	936	45278	dark green

SYMBOL	BEAD		COLOR
♥	02012	Mill Hill Seed Bead	Royal Plum
U	02019	Mill Hill Seed Bead	Crystal Honey
5	02024	Mill Hill Seed Bead	Heather Mauve
■	02049	Mill Hill Seed Bead	Dark Basil
◉	03062	Mill Hill Seed Bead	Blue Velvet
▭		2mm bugle bead*	dark green

*Two Dark Basil seed beads may be used in place of each bugle bead.

Mallow

The design, shown on page 13, was stitched over 2 fabric threads on a 7" x 7" piece of Zweigart® Cream Cashel Linen® (28 count). The design size is 2³/₄" x 2³/₄". Beads were attached using 2 strands of floss that matches the fabric. The design was framed in a 3¹/₂" x 3¹/₂" purchased frame.

Stitch Count:
(37w x 37h)

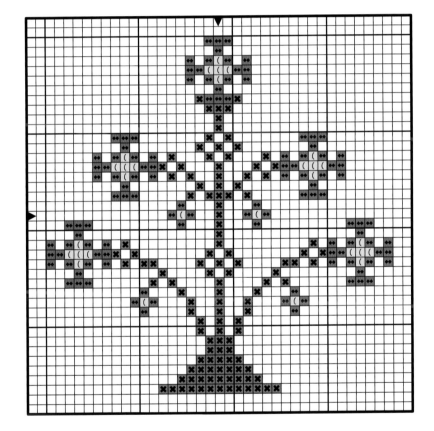

FLOSS SUBSTITUTION KEY

To stitch this design in floss only, replace each seed bead with a Cross Stitch. Use 2 strands of floss.

SYMBOL	DMC	SUL
✖	936	45278
(	3822	45419
◆◆	3712	45362

SYMBOL	MILL HILL	COLOR	QUANTITY
✖	00374 Seed Bead	Rainbow	120
(	02105 Seed Bead	Sweet Corn	29
◆◆	03057 Seed Bead	Cherry Sorbet	116

Stitch Count:
With border (55w x 82h)
Without border (43w x 68h)

Peony

The design, shown on page 13, was stitched over 2 fabric threads on a 10" x 12" piece of Zweigart® Raw Cashel Linen® (28 count). The design size is 4" x 5⅞" and was framed in a 5" x 7" purchased frame. The design, shown on left, was also stitched without the border on a 9½" x 11" piece of Zweigart® Flax Cashel Linen® (28 count). The design size is 3⅛" x 4⅞" and it was framed in a 4" x 6" purchased frame. Beads were attached using 2 strands of floss that matches the fabric. If desired, Backstitch the stitcher's name and year stitched using 1 strand of floss in desired color and the small alphabet on page 56.

WITH BORDER

SYMBOL	MILL HILL	COLOR	QUANTITY
■	00081 Seed Bead	Jet	400
e	02012 Seed Bead	Royal Plum	580
▲	02020 Seed Bead	Creme de Mint	317
╱	02024 Seed Bead	Heather Mauve	328

WITHOUT BORDER

SYMBOL	MILL HILL	COLOR	QUANTITY
■	00081 Seed Bead	Jet	186
▲	00332 Seed Bead	Emerald	317
╱	02024 Seed Bead	Heather Mauve	186
e	60367 Seed Bead	Frosted Garnet	334

FLOSS SUBSTITUTION KEY

To stitch this design in floss only, replace each seed bead with a Cross Stitch. Use 2 strands of floss.

WITH BORDER

SYMBOL	DMC	SUL
■	3799	45397
e	3803	45400
▲	909	45257
╱	3042	45327

WITHOUT BORDER

SYMBOL	DMC	SUL
■	3799	45397
▲	890	45243
╱	3042	45327
e	814	45216

The Vineyard

The design, shown on page 14, was stitched over 2 fabric threads on a 12¹/₂" x 20¹/₂" piece of Zweigart® Summer Khaki Cashel Linen® (28 count). The design size is 6³/₈" x 14³/₈". Two strands of floss were used for Cross Stitch. Beads were attached using 2 strands of floss that matches the fabric. If desired, Backstitch the stitcher's name and year stitched using 1 strand of floss in desired color and the small alphabet on page 56. The design was custom framed.

X	DMC	SUL	COLOR
	501	45110	teal

SYMBOL	MILL HILL		COLOR	QUANTITY
	02012 Seed Bead		Royal Plum	796
	02023 Seed Bead		Root Beer	277
	03034 Seed Bead		Royal Amethyst	660
	03035 Seed Bead		Royal Green	575
	03053 Seed Bead		Purple Passion	530
	03055 Seed Bead		Bay Leaf	554
	62031 Seed Bead		Frosted Gold	308
	72051 Small Bugle Beads		Royal Mauve	34

Indicates repeated row

Stitch Count:
(89w x 201h)

FLOSS SUBSTITUTION KEY

To stitch this design in floss only, replace each seed bead with a Cross Stitch. Replace each bugle bead with 4 Cross Stitches or 3 Straight Stitches. Use 2 strands of floss.

SYMBOL	DMC	SUL
	501	45110
	3803	45400
	975	45304
	550	45123
	500	45109
	3746	45373
	503	45112
	676	45156
	3041	45326

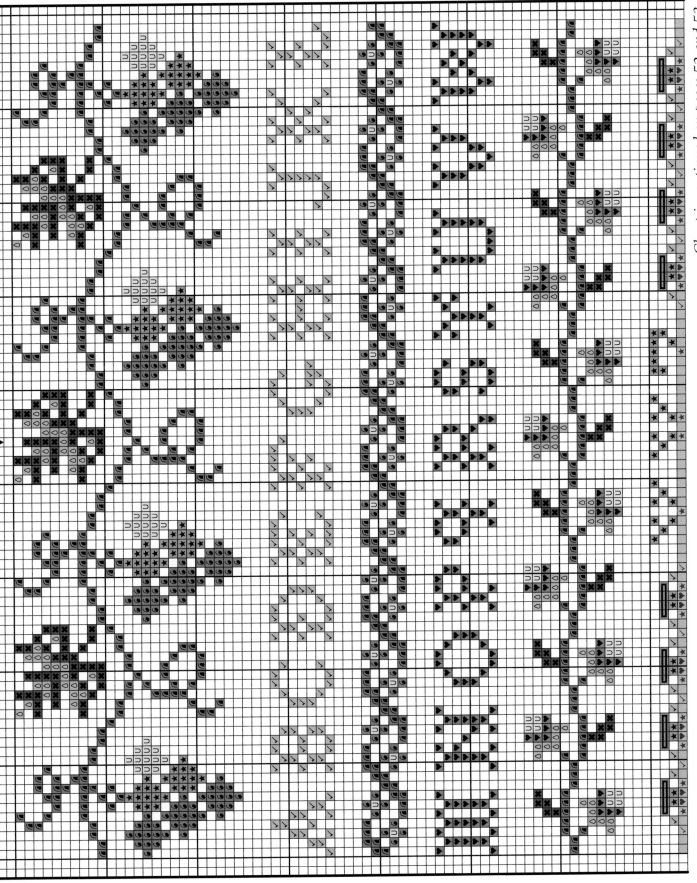

Chart is continued on pages 52 and 53.

*The Vineyard
(continued
from page 51)*

SYMBOL	X	DMC	SUL	COLOR
	501	45110	teal
		MILL HILL		COLOR
	02012 Seed Bead			Royal Plum
	02023 Seed Bead			Root Beer
	03034 Seed Bead			Royal Amethyst
	03035 Seed Bead			Royal Green
	03053 Seed Bead			Purple Passion
	03055 Seed Bead			Bay Leaf
	62031 Seed Bead			Frosted Gold
	72051 Small Bugle Beads			Royal Mauve
	Indicates repeated row			

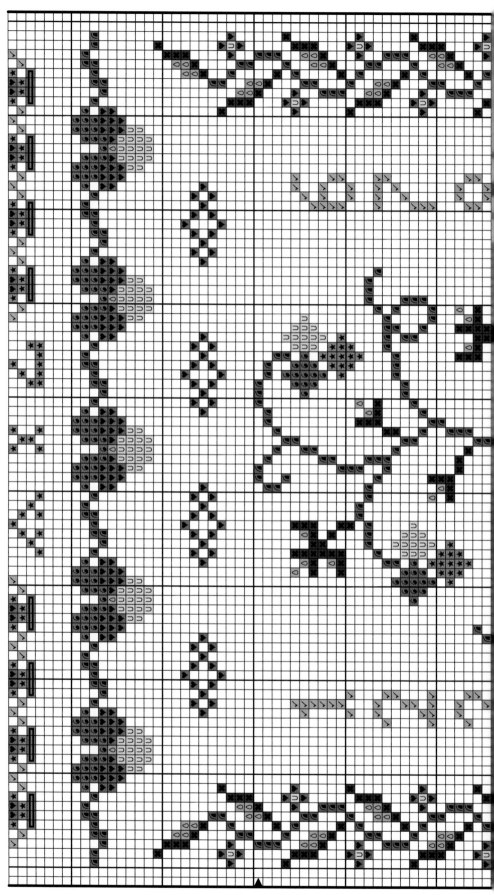

Waterlily

The design, shown on page 15, was stitched over 2 fabric threads on a 12" x 16" piece of Zweigart® Flax Cashel Linen® (28 count). The design size is 5³/₄" x 9³/₄". Two strands of floss were used for Cross Stitch. Dark Basil beads were attached using 2 strands of dark green floss. All other beads were attached using 2 strands of floss that matches the fabric. If desired, Backstitch the stitcher's name and year stitched using 1 strand of floss in desired color and the small alphabet on page 56. The design was custom framed.

X	DMC	SUL	COLOR
✖	936	45278	dark green

SYMBOL	BEAD		COLOR	QUANTITY
▶	02012	Mill Seed Bead	Royal Plum	600
U	02019	Mill Hill Seed Bead	Crystal Honey	236
5	02024	Mill Hill Seed Bead	Heather Mauve	397
■	02049	Mill Hill Seed Bead	Dark Basil	987
◑	03062	Mill Hill Seed Bead	Blue Velvet	221
▯	2mm bugle bead*		dark green	44
	Indicates repeated row			

*Two Dark Basil seed beads may be used in place of each bugle bead.

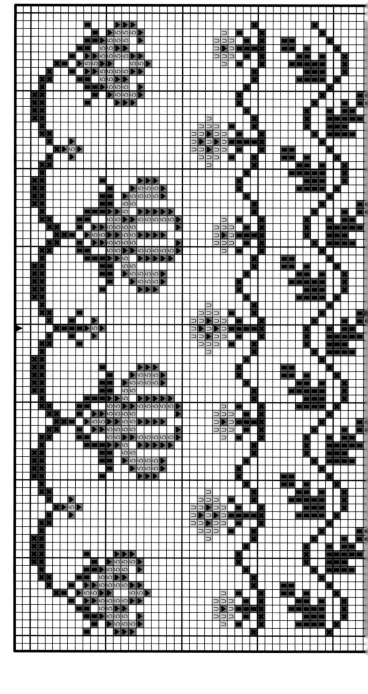

Stitch Count:
(79w x 135h)